The Training of a Forester

THE TRAINING OF A FORESTER

FOURTH EDITION

THE TRAINING OF
A FORESTER

BY
GIFFORD PINCHOT

REVISED THIRD EDITION

WITH EIGHT ILLUSTRATIONS

PHILADELPHIA & LONDON
J. B. LIPPINCOTT COMPANY

PRINTED BY J. B. LIPPINCOTT COMPANY
AT THE WASHINGTON SQUARE PRESS
PHILADELPHIA, U.S.A.

To

OVERTON W. PRICE
FRIEND AND FELLOW WORKER

TO WHOM IS DUE, MORE THAN TO ANY OTHER MAN, THE
HIGH EFFICIENCY OF THE UNITED STATES FOREST SERVICE

PREFACE

AT one time or another, the largest question before every young man is, "What shall I do with my life?" Among the possible openings, which best suits his ambition, his tastes, and his capacities? Along what line shall he undertake to make a successful career? The search for a life work and the choice of one is surely as important business as can occupy a boy verging into manhood. It is to help in the decision of those who are considering forestry as a profession that this little book has been written.

To the young man who is attracted to forestry and begins to consider it as a possible profession, certain questions present themselves. What is forestry? If he takes it up, what will his work be, and where? Does it in fact offer the satisfying type of

outdoor life which it appears to offer? What
chance does it present for a successful career,
for a career of genuine usefulness, and what
is the chance to make a living? Is he fitted
for it in character, mind, and body? If so,
what training does he need? These questions deserve an answer.

To the men whom it really suits, forestry
offers a career more attractive, it may be
said in all fairness, than any other career
whatsoever. I doubt if any other profession
can show a membership so uniformly and
enthusiastically in love with the work. The
men who have taken it up, practised it, and
left it for other work are few. But to the
man not fully adapted for it, forestry must
be punishment, pure and simple. Those who
have begun the study of forestry, and then
have learned that it was not for them, have
doubtless been more in number than those
who have followed it through.

6

PREFACE

I urge no man to make forestry his profession, but rather to keep away from it if he can. In forestry a man is either altogether at home or very much out of place. Unless he has a compelling love for the Forester's life and the Forester's work, let him keep out of it.

January, 1914.   G. P.

PREFACE TO THIRD EDITION

For this third edition, the facts and figures throughout have been revised and brought up to date, and a new chapter containing some essential information about our forests has been added. Special acknowledgment is due to Mr. Herbert A. Smith, Editor of the U. S. Forest Service, for his unwearied assistance both in the work of revision and in the new chapter.

G. P.

Milford, Pa.

CONTENTS

ILLUSTRATIONS

THE TRAINING OF A FORESTER

WHAT IS A FOREST?

FIRST, What is forestry? Forestry is the knowledge of the forest. In particular, it is the art of handling the forest so that it will render whatever service is required of it without being impoverished or destroyed. For example, a forest may be handled so as to produce saw logs, telegraph poles, barrel hoops, firewood, tan bark, or turpentine. The main purpose of its treatment may be to prevent the washing of soil, to regulate the flow of streams, to support cattle or sheep, or it may be handled so as to supply a wide range and combination of uses. Forestry is the art of producing from the forest whatever it can yield for the service of man.

THE TRAINING OF A FORESTER

Before we can understand forestry, certain facts about the forest itself must be kept in mind. A forest is not a mere collection of individual trees, just as a city is not a mere collection of unrelated men and women, or a Nation like ours merely a certain number of independent racial groups. A forest, like a city, is a complex community with a life of its own. It has a soil and an atmosphere of its own, chemically and physically different from any other, with plants and shrubs as well as trees which are peculiar to it. It has a resident population of insects and higher animals entirely distinct from that outside. Most important of all, from the Forester's point of view, the members of the forest live in an exact and intricate system of competition and mutual assistance, of help or harm, which extends to all the inhabitants of this complicated city of trees.

14

THE TRAINING OF A FORESTER

The trees in a forest are all helped by mutually protecting each other against high winds, and by producing a richer and moister soil than would be possible if the trees stood singly and apart. They compete among themselves by their roots for moisture in the soil, and for light and space by the growth of their crowns in height and breadth. Perhaps the strongest weapon which trees have against each other is growth in height. In certain species intolerant of shade, the tree which is overtopped has lost the race for good. The number of young trees which destroy each other in this fierce struggle for existence is prodigious, so that often a few score per acre are all that survive to middle or old age out of many tens of thousands of seedlings which entered the race of life on approximately even terms.

Not only has a forest a character of its own, which arises from the fact that it is a

15

community of trees, but each species of tree
has peculiar characteristics and habits also.
Just as in New York City, for example, the
French, the Germans, the Italians, the Hun-
garians, and the Chinese each have quarters
of their own, and in those quarters live in
accordance with habits which distinguish
each race from all the others, so the different
species of pines and hemlocks, oaks and
maples prefer and are found in certain definite types of locality, and live in accordance with definite racial habits which are as
general and unfailing as the racial characteristics which distinguish, for example,
the Italians from the Germans, or the
Swedes from the Chinese.

The most important of these characteristics of race or species are those which are
concerned with the relation of each to light,
heat, and moisture. Thus, a river birch will
die if it has only as much water as will suffice

to keep a post oak in the best condition, and the warm climate in which the balsam fir would perish is just suited to the requirements of a long leaf pine or a magnolia.

The tolerance of a tree for shade may vary greatly at different times of its life, but a white pine always requires more light than a hemlock, and a beech throughout its life will flourish with less sunshine or reflected light than, for example, an oak or a tulip tree.

Trees are limited in their distribution also by their adaptability, in which they vary greatly. Thus a bald cypress will grow both in wetter and in dryer land than an oak; a red cedar will flourish from Florida to the Canadian line, while other species, like the Eastern larch, the Western mountain hemlock, or the big trees of California, are confined in their native localities within extremely narrow limits.

THE TRAINING OF A FORESTER

THE FORESTER'S KNOWLEDGE

THE trained Forester must know the forest as a doctor knows the human machine. First of all, he must be able to distinguish the different trees of which the forest is composed, for that is like learning to read. He must know the way they are made and the way they grow; but far more important than all else, he must base his knowledge upon that part of forestry which is called Silvics, the knowledge of the relation of trees to light, heat, and moisture, to the soil, and to each other.

The well-trained Forester must also know the forest shrubs and at least the more important smaller forest plants, something of the insect and animal life of his domain, and the birds and fish. He must have a good working knowledge of rocks, soils, and streams, and of the methods of making

18

roads, trails, and bridges. He should be an expert in woodcraft, able to travel the forest safely and surely by day or by night. It is essential that he should have a knowledge of the theory and the practice of lumbering, and he should know something about lumber markets and the value of lumber, about surveying and map making, and many other matters which are considered more at length in the Chapter on Training. There are as yet in America comparatively few men who have acquired even fairly well the more important knowledge which should be included in the training of a Forester.

THE FOREST AND THE NATION

THE position of the forest in the housekeeping of any nation is unlike that of any other great natural resource, for the forest not only furnishes wood, without which civilization as we know it would be impossible, but serves also to protect or make valuable many of the other things without which we could not get on. Thus the forest cover protects the soil from the effects of wind, and holds it in place. For lack of it hundreds of thousands of square miles have been converted by the winds from moderately fertile, productive land to arid drifting sands. Narrow strips of forest planted as windbreaks make agriculture possible in certain regions by preventing destruction of crops by moisture-stealing dry winds which so afflict the central portions of our country.

Without the forests the great bulk of our mining for coal, metals, and the precious minerals would be either impossible or vastly more expensive than it is at present, because the galleries of mines are propped with wood, and so protected against caving in. So far, no satisfactory substitute for the wooden railroad tie has been devised; and our whole system of land transportation is directly dependent for its existence upon the forest, which supplies more than one hundred and twenty million new railroad ties every year in the United States alone.

The forest regulates and protects the flow of streams. Its effect is to reduce the height of floods and to moderate extremes of low water. The official measurements of the United States Geological Survey have finally settled this long-disputed question. By protecting mountain slopes against excessive soil wash, it protects also the lowlands upon which this wash would otherwise be deposited and the rivers whose channels it would clog. It is well within the truth to say that the utility of any system of rivers for transportation, for irrigation, for water-power, and for domestic supply depends in great part upon the protection which forests offer to the headwaters of the streams, and that without such protection none of these uses can be expected long to endure.

Of the two basic materials of our civilization, iron and wood, the forest supplies one. The dominant place of the forest in our national economy is well illustrated by the fact that no article whatsoever, whether of use or ornament, whether it be for food, shelter, clothing, convenience, protection, or decoration, can be produced and delivered to the user, as industry is now organized, without the help of the forest in supplying wood. An examination of the history of any article, including the production of the raw material, and its manufacture, transportation, and distribution, will at once make this point clear.

The forest is a national necessity. Without the material, the protection, and the assistance it supplies, no nation can long succeed. Many regions of the old world, such as Palestine, Greece, Northern Africa, and Central India, offer in themselves the most impressive object lessons of the effect upon national prosperity and national character of the neglect of the forest and its consequent destruction.

THE FORESTER'S POINT OF VIEW

THE central idea of the Forester, in handling the forest, is to promote and perpetuate its greatest use to men. His purpose is to make it serve the greatest good of the greatest number for the longest time. Before the members of any other profession dealing with natural resources, the Foresters acquired the long look ahead. This was only natural, because in forestry it is seldom that a man lives to harvest the crop which he helped to sow. The Forester must look forward, because the natural resource with which he deals matures so slowly, and because, if steps are to be taken to insure for succeeding generations a supply of the things the forest yields, they must be taken long in advance. The idea of using the forest first for the greatest good of the present generation, and then for the greatest good of succeeding generations through the long future of the nation and the race— that is the Forester's point of view.

'The use of foresight to insure the existence of the forest in the future, and, so far as practicable, the continued or increasing abundance of its service to men, naturally suggested the use of foresight in the same way as to other natural resources as well. Thus it was the Forester's point of view, applied not only to the forest but to the lands, the minerals, and the streams, which produced the Conservation policy. The idea

24

of applying foresight and common-sense to
the other natural resources as well as to the
forest was natural and inevitable. It works
out, equally as a matter of course, into the
conception of a planned and orderly development of all that the earth contains for
the uses of men. This leads in turn to the
application of the same principle to other
questions and resources. It was foreseen
from the beginning by those who were responsible for inaugurating the Conservation
movement that its natural development
would in time work out into a planned and
orderly scheme for national efficiency, based
on the elimination of waste, and directed
toward the best use of all we have for the
greatest good of the greatest number for the
longest time. It is easy to see that this
principle (the Forester's principle, first
brought to public attention by Foresters) is
the key to national success.

THE TRAINING OF A FORESTER

Forestry, then, is seen to be peculiarly essential to the national prosperity, both now and hereafter. National degradation and decay have uniformly followed the excessive destruction of forests by other nations, and will inevitably become our portion if we continue to destroy our forests three times faster than they are produced, as we are doing now. The principles of forestry, therefore, must occupy a commanding place in determining the future prosperity or failure of our nation, and this commanding position in the field of ideas is naturally and properly reflected in the dignity and high standing which the profession of forestry, young as it is, has already acquired in the United States. This position it must be the first care of every member of the profession to maintain and increase.

In the long run, no profession rises higher than the degree of public consideration which marks its members. The profession of forestry is in many ways a peculiarly responsible profession, but in nothing more so than in its vital connection with the whole future welfare of our country and in the obligation which lies upon its members to see that its reputation and standing, which are the measures of its capacity for usefulness, are kept strong and clear.

THE ESTABLISHMENT OF FORESTRY

IN the United States, forestry is passing out of the pioneer phase of agitation and the education of public opinion, and into the permanent phase of the practice of the profession. The first steps in forestry in this country, as in any other where the development and destruction of natural resources has been rapid, were necessarily directed mainly to informing the public mind upon the importance of forestry, and to building up national and State laws and organizations for the protection of timberlands set aside for the public benefit. The right to be heard with respect by the men who were already in control of the larger part of our total forest wealth had to be won, and has been won. What is more, in the teeth of the bitterest opposition of private special interests, the right of the public to first consideration in the protection and development of the forest and of all the resources it contains had to be asserted and established. That has now been done.

In the United States these steps in the movement for the wise use of the forest have been taken mainly in the last dozen or fifteen years, during which the Federal forest organization has grown from an insignificant division of less than a dozen men to the

present United States Forest Service, of
more than three thousand members. During
this period, also, forestry, both as a profession and as a public necessity, has won en-
during public recognition, and at the same
time more public timberland has been set
aside for the public use and to remain in
the public hands than during all the rest of
our history put together. To-day the National Forests are reasonably safe in the
protection of public opinion, not against all
attack, it is true, but against any successful
attempt to dismember and turn them over
to the special interests who already control
the bulk and the best of our forests. The
public has accepted forestry as necessary to
the public welfare, both in the present and
in the future; State forest organizations are
springing up; forestry has won the right to
be heard in the business offices as well as in
the conventions of the private owners of

forest land; and the time for the practice of
the profession has fully come.

THE WORK OF A FORESTER

WHAT does a Forester do? I will try to
answer this question, first, with reference to
the United States Forest Service, and later
as to the numerous other fields of activity
which are opening or have already opened
to the trained Forester in the United States.

THE FOREST SERVICE

THE United States Forest Service is responsible both for the general progress of
forestry, so far as the United States Government is concerned, and for the protection
and use of the National Forests. These
National Forests now cover a net area of one
hundred and fifty-five million acres, or as
much land as is included in all the New

THE TRAINING OF A FORESTER

England States, with New York, Pennsylvania, New Jersey, Delaware, Maryland, Virginia and West Virginia. The head of the Service, whose official title is " Forester," is charged with the great task of protecting this vast area against fire, theft, and other depredations, and of making all its resources, the wood, water, and grass, the minerals, and the soil, available and useful to the people of the United States under regulations which will secure development and prevent destruction or waste.

The United States Forest Service consists, first, of a protective force of Forest Guards and Forest Rangers, who spend practically the whole of their time in the forest; second, of an executive staff of Forest Supervisors and their assistants, who have immediate charge of the handling of the National Forests; and third, of an administrative staff divided between headquarters

31

in Washington and the seven local administrative offices, six in the West, where the National Forests mainly lie, and one in the East.

The work of a Forest Ranger is, first of all, to protect the District committed to his charge against fire. That comes before all else. For that purpose, the Ranger patrols his District during the seasons when fires are dangerous, or watches for signs of fire from certain high points, called fire-lookouts, or both. He keeps the trails and fire lines clear and the telephone in working order, and sees to it that the fire fighting tools, such as spades, axes, and rakes, are in good condition and ready for service. If he is wise, he establishes such relations with the people who live in his neighborhood that they become his volunteer assistants in watching for forest fires, in taking precautions against them, and in notifying him of them when they do take place.

STRINGING A FOREST TELEPHONE LINE

THE TRAINING OF A FORESTER

Fighting a forest fire in some respects is like fighting a fire in a city. In both, the first and most necessary thing is to get men and apparatus to the site of the fire at the first practicable moment. For this purpose, fire-engines and men are always ready in the city, while in the forest the telephones, trails, and bridges must be kept in condition, and the forest officers must be ready to move instantly day or night.

It is far better to prevent a forest fire from starting than to have to put it out after it has started; but in spite of all the care that can be exercised with the means at hand, many fires start. Each year the Forest Service men extinguish about forty-five hundred fires, nearly all of them while they are still small. At times, however, when the woods are very dry and the wind blows hard, in spite of all that can be done, a fire will grow large enough to be dangerous not only to the forest but to human life. Thus in the summer of 1910, the driest ever known in certain parts of the West, high winds drove the forest fires clear beyond the control of the fire fighters, many of whom were compelled to fight for their own lives.

The worst of these fires were in Montana and Idaho, where the whole power of the Forest Service was used against them. The Forest Rangers, under the orders of their Supervisors, immediately organized or took charge of small companies of fire fighters, and began the work of getting them under control. But so fierce was the wind and so terrible the heat of the fires and the speed with which they moved, that in many places it became a question of saving the lives of the fire fighters rather than of putting out the fires. As a matter of fact, nearly a hundred of the men temporarily employed to help the Government fire fighters lost their lives, and many more would have died but for the courage, resource, and knowledge of the woods of the Forest Rangers.

Take, for example, the case of Ranger Edward C. Pulaski, of the Cœur d'Alene National Forest, stationed at Wallace, Idaho. Pulaski had charge of forty Italians and Poles. He had been at work with them for many hours, when the flames grew to be so threatening that it became a question of whether he could save his men. The fire was travelling faster than the men could make their way through the dense forest, and the only hope was to find some place into which the fire could not come. Accordingly Pulaski guided his party at a run through the blinding smoke to an abandoned mine he knew of in the neighborhood. When they reached it, he sent the men into the workings ahead of him, hung a wet blanket across the mouth of the tunnel, and himself stood there on guard. The fierce heat, the stifling air, and their deadly fear drove some of the foreigners temporarily insane, and a number of them tried to break out. With drawn revolver Pulaski held them back. One man did get by him and was burned to death. Many fainted in the tunnel. The Ranger himself, more exposed than any of his men, was terribly burned. He stood at his post, however, for five hours, until the fire had passed, and brought his party through without losing a single man except that one who got out of the tunnel, although his own injuries were so severe that he was in the hospital for two months as a result of them. The record of the Forest Service in these terrible fires is one of which every Forester may well be proud.

The Ranger must protect his District, not only against fire but against the theft of timber and the incessant efforts of land grabbers to steal Government lands. To prevent the theft of timber is usually not difficult, but it is far harder to prevent fake homesteaders, fraudulent mining men, and other dishonest claimants from seizing upon land to which they have no right, and so preventing honest men from using these claims to make a living.

In the past, this problem has presented the most serious difficulties, and still occasionally does so. There is no louder shouter for "justice" than a balked habitual land thief with political influence behind him. To illustrate the kind of attack upon the Forest Service to which fraudulent land claims have constantly given rise, I may cite the statements made during one of the annual attempts in the Senate to break down the Service. One of the Senators asserted that in his State the Forest Service was overbearing and tyrannical, and that in a particular case it had driven out of his home a citizen known to the Senator, and had left him and his family to wander houseless upon the hillside, and that for no good reason whatsoever.

This statement, if it had been true, would at once have destroyed the standing of the Service in the minds of many of its friends, and would have led to immediate defeat in the fight then going on. Fortunately, the records of the Service were so complete, and the knowledge of field conditions on the part of the men in Washington was so thorough, that the mere mention of the general locality of the supposed outrage by the Senator made it easy to identify the individual case. The man in question, instead of being an honest settler with a wife and family, was the keeper of a disreputable saloon and dance hall, a well-known law-breaker whom the local authorities had tried time and again to dispossess and drive away. But by means of his fraudulent claim the man had always defeated the local officers. When, however, the officers of the Forest Service took the case in hand, the situation changed and things moved quickly. The disreputable saloon was promptly removed from the fraudulent land claim by means of which the keeper of it had held on, and this thoroughly undesirable citizen either went out of business or removed his abominable trade to some locality outside the National Forest.

The actual facts were fully brought out in the debate next day, remained uncontradicted, and saved the fight for the Forest Service. The whole incident may be found at length in the Congressional Record.

The Forest Ranger is charged with overseeing and regulating the free use of timber by settlers and others who live in or near the National Forests. Last year (1916) the

Forest Service gave away without charge more than 120 million board feet of saw timber, logs, fencing, fuel, and other material to men and women who needed it for their own use. Usually it is the Ranger's work to issue the permits for this free use, and to designate the timber that may be cut. For this purpose, he must be well acquainted with the kinds and the uses of the trees in his District, and it is most important that he should know something of how their reproduction can best be secured, in order that the free use may be permitted without injury to the future welfare of the forest.

A Ranger oversees the use of his District for the grazing of cattle, sheep, and other domestic animals. He must acquaint himself with the brands and marks of the various owners, and should be well posted in the essentials of the business of raising cattle, sheep, and horses. The allotment of graz-

ing areas is one of the most difficult problems
to adjust, because the demand is almost
always for much more range than is available and the division of what range there is
among the local owners of stock often pre-
sents serious difficulties; in which the
Ranger's local knowledge and advice is constantly sought by his superior officer.

There is a wise law, passed at the request
of the Forest Service, under which land in
the National Forests which is shown to be
agricultural may be entered under the home-
stead law, and used for the making of homes.
This law is peculiarly hard to carry out because the ceaseless efforts of land grabbers
to misuse it demand great vigilance on the
part of the Forest Officers. In many cases
it is the Ranger who makes the report upon
which the decision as to the agricultural or
non-agricultural character of the land is
based, although in other cases the examina-

tions to determine whether the land is really agricultural in character are made by Examiners especially trained for this duty. Serious controversies into which politics enter are often caused by the efforts of speculators and others, under pretext of this law, to get possession of lands chiefly valuable for their timber.

The building and maintenance of trails, telephone lines, roads, bridges, and fences in his District is under the charge of the Ranger, and in many cases Rangers and Forest Guards are appointed by the State as Wardens to see to it that the game and fish laws are properly enforced.

Next to the protection of his District from fire, the most important duty of the Ranger has to do with the sale of timber and the marking of the individual trees which are to be cut. The reproduction of the forest depends directly on what trees are kept for

seed, or on how the existing young growth is protected and preserved in felling and swamping the trees which have been marked for cutting, and in skidding the logs. The disposal of the slash must be looked after, for it has much to do with forest reproduction, and with promoting safety from fire. Then, the scaling of the logs determines the amount of the payment the Government receives for its timber, and there are often regulations governing the transportation of the scaled logs whose enforcement is of great consequence to the future forest.

Nearly all of these duties the Ranger may perform in certain cases without supervision, if his judgment and training are sufficient, but the marking especially is often done under the eye or in accordance with the directions of the technical Forester, whose duty it is to see that the future of the forest is protected by enforcing the conditions of sale.

43

THE TRAINING OF A FORESTER

These are but a part of the duties of the Ranger, for he is concerned with all the uses which his District may serve. The streams, for example, may be important for city water supply, irrigation, or for waterpower, and their use for these purposes must be under his eye. Hotels and saw-mills on sites leased from the Government may dot his District here and there. The land within National Forests may be put to a thousand other uses, from a bee ranch on the Cleveland Forest in southern California to a whaling station on the Tongass Forest in Alaska, all of which means work for him.

The result of all this is that the Ranger comes in contact with city dwellers, irrigators, cattlemen, sheepmen, and horsemen, ranchers, storekeepers, hotel men, hunters, miners, and lumbermen, and above all with the settlers who live in or near his District. With all these it is his duty to keep on good terms, for well he knows that one man at certain times can set more fires than a regiment can extinguish, and that the best protection for his District comes from the friendly interest of the men who live in it or near it.

A Forest Guard is in effect an assistant to the Ranger, and may be called upon to carry out most of the duties which fall upon a Ranger.

The foregoing short statement will make it clear that preliminary experience as a Ranger may be of the utmost value to the man who proposes later on to perform in the Government Service the duties of a trained Forester. It is becoming more and more common, and fortunately so, for graduates of forest schools to begin their work in the United States Forest Service as Rangers or Forest Guards. The man who has done well a Ranger's work, like the graduate of an engineering school who, after graduation, has entered a machine shop as a hand, has acquired a body of practical information and experience which will be invaluable to him in the later practice of his profession, and which is far beyond the reach of any man who has not been trained in the actual execution of this work on the ground and in actual daily contact with the multifarious uses and users of the forest.

THE FOREST SUPERVISOR

THE Supervisor is the general manager of a National Forest. The responsibility for the protection, care, and use of it falls upon him, under the direction of the District Forester. The Supervisor is responsible for making the use of his forest as valuable and as convenient as possible for the people in and around the area of which he has charge.

He deals with the organizations of forest users, such as local stock associations, and issues permits for grazing live stock in the forest. Permits for cutting small amounts of timber are granted by him, and he advertises in the papers the sale of larger amounts and receives bids from prospective purchasers; keeps the accounts of his forest; and makes regular reports on a variety of important subjects, such as the personnel of his forest force, the permanent improvements made or to be made, the permits issued for regular and special uses of the forest and for free use of timber and forage, the number and kinds of predatory animals killed, the amount of forest planting accomplished, and the expense and losses from forest fires. He has general oversight of the roads, trails, and other improvements on his forest; and prepares plans for the extension of them. In particular, he directs, controls, and inspects

47

the work of the Ranger and Guards, and in general, he attends to the thousand and one matters which go to adjusting the use of the forest to the needs of the men who use it, and on which depends whether the forest is well or badly thought of among the people whose coöperation or opposition have so much to do with making its management successful or otherwise.

The Supervisor spends about half his time in the office and half in the field, inspecting the work of his men and consulting with them, meeting local residents or associations of local residents who have propositions to submit for improving the service of the forest to them, or for correcting mistakes, or who wish to lay before the Supervisor some one of the numberless matters in which the forest affects their welfare. The usefulness of the Supervisor depends as much upon his good judgment, his ability to meet men and do business with them, and his knowledge of local needs and local affairs, as it does upon his knowledge of the forest itself. As in the case of every superior officer, his attitude toward his work, his energy, his good sense, and his good will are or should be reflected in the men under him, so that his position is one of the greatest importance in determining the success or failure of each National Forest, and hence of the Forest Service as a whole. More and more of the trained Foresters in the Service are seeking and securing appointments as Forest Supervisors because of the interest and satisfaction they find in the work. Such men handle both the professional and business sides of forest management. Many of their duties, therefore, are described in the succeeding chapter.

The position of Supervisor is in many respects the most desirable a trained Forester can occupy in the Forest Service, and the most responsible of the field positions.

THE TRAINED FORESTER

To each forest where timber cutting has become important there are assigned one or more Forest Assistants or Forest Examiners. These are professionally trained Foresters. They are subordinate upon each forest to the Supervisor as manager, but it is their work which has most to do with deciding whether the Forest Service in general is to be successful or is to fail in the great task of preserving the forest by wise use.

The Forest Assistant secures his position with the Service by passing an examination devised to test his technical knowledge and his ability. After he has served two years as Forest Assistant the quality and quantity of his work will have determined his fitness

50

to continue in the employ of the Government. If he is unfit he may be dropped, for there are many young and ambitious men ready to step into his place. If he makes good he is promoted to the grade of Forest Examiner and is put definitely in charge of certain lines of professional work; always, of course, under the direction of the Supervisor, of whom he becomes the adviser on all problems involving technical forestry.

The most important tasks of the trained Forester on a National Forest are the preparation of working plans for the use of the forest by methods which will protect and perpetuate it as well, and the carrying out of the plans when made. This is forestry in the technical sense of the word. It involves a thorough study of the kinds of timber, their amount and location, their rate of growth, their value, the ease or difficulty of their reproduction, and the methods by which the timber can be cut at a profit and at the same time the reproduction of the forest can be safely secured. A working plan usually includes a considerable number of maps, which often have to be drawn in the first place from actual surveys on the ground by the Forest Examiner. These maps contain the information secured by working-plan studies, and are of the first necessity for the wise and skilful handling of the forest. They often constitute, also, most important documents in the history of its condition and use.

On many of the National Forests the need for immediate use of the timber is so urgent and so just that there is no time to prepare elaborate working plans. Timber sales must be made, and made at once; but they must be made, nevertheless, in a way that will fully protect the future welfare of the forest. Whether working plans can be prepared or not, a most important duty of the technical

THE TRAINING OF A FORESTER

Forester is to work out the conditions under which a given body of timber can be cut with safety to the forest, especially with safety to its reproduction and future growth. The principal study for a timber sale will usually include an examination of the general features and condition of the forest, and the determination of the diameter down to which it is advisable to cut the standing trees, a diameter which must be fixed at such a size as will protect the forest and make the lumbering pay. It will include also an investigation, more or less thorough and complete, as the conditions warrant, of the silvical habits of one or more of the species of trees in that forest. The areas which form natural units for the logging and transportation of the timber must be worked out and laid off, and careful estimates, or measurements, of the amount of standing timber and of its value on the stump must be made, as well as of the cost of moving it to the mill or to the railroad.

The Forest Examiner must also consider, in many cases, the building of logging roads or railroads, timber slides, etc., and must make a careful study of the material into which the trees to be cut can best be worked up, and of the value of such material in the market. Most of all, however, he must study, think over, and decide what he will recommend as to the conditions which are to govern the logging conditions by which the protection of the forest is to be insured. These conditions, fixed by his superiors upon the report of the Forest Examiner, determine whether an individual timber sale is forestry or forest destruction. This is the central question in the administration of the National Forests from the national point of view.

The principal objects of the conditions

laid down for a timber sale are always the reproduction of the forest and its safety
against fire. Natural reproduction from
self-sown seed is almost invariably the result
desired; and so the question of the seed trees
to be left, and how they are to be located or
spaced, is fundamental, unless there is ample
young growth already on the ground. In
the latter case this young growth must not
be smashed or bent by throwing the older
trees on top of it, or against it, and the young
saplings bent down by the felled tops must
be promptly released.

In order to avoid danger to the young
growth already present or to be secured, as
well as to protect the older trees from fires,
the slash produced in lumbering, the tops
lopped from the trees up to and beyond the
highest point to which the lumbermen are
required to take the logs, must be satisfac-
torily disposed of—either by scattering it

thinly over the ground, by piling and burning, or often by piling alone.

These and many other conditions of sale must be studied out in a form adapted to each particular case, and must be discussed with the men who propose to buy, who often have wise and practical suggestions to make.

Similar questions on a less important scale present themselves and must be answered in the matter of small timber sales, and of timber given without charge under free-use permits to settlers and others.

When the terms of a contract of sale have been worked out and accepted and the timber has been sold, then the Forest Assistant has charge of the extremely interesting task of marking the trees that are to be cut, in accordance with these terms. Usually this is done by marking all the trees which are to be felled, but sometimes by marking only the trees which are to remain.

THE TRAINING OF A FORESTER

The marking is usually done by blazing each tree and stamping the letters " U. S." upon the blaze with a Government marking axe or hatchet. It must be done in such a way that the loggers will have no excuse either for cutting an unmarked tree or leaving a marked tree uncut, or *vice versa,* as the case may be. The marking may be carried out by the Rangers and Forest Guards under supervision of the Forest Assistant, or in difficult situations he may mark or direct the marking of each tree himself. Marking is fascinating work.

Later, while the logging is under way, the Forest Examiner will often inspect it to see that the terms of the sale are complied with, that the trees cut are thrown in places where they will not unduly damage either young growth or the larger trees which are to remain, and that the other conditions laid down for the logging in the contract of sale are observed. The scaling of the logs to determine the amount of payment to the Government will many times be under his supervision, although in the larger sales this work, as well as the routine inspection of the logging, is usually carried out by a special body of expert lumbermen, who often bring to it a much wider knowledge of the woods than the men in actual charge of the lumbering.

In nearly every National Forest there are areas upon which the trees have been destroyed by fire. Many of these are so large or so remote from seed-bearing trees that natural reproduction will not suffice to replace the forest. In such localities planting is needed, and for that purpose the Forest Examiner must establish and conduct a forest nursery. The decision on the kind of trees to plant and on the methods of raising and planting them, the collection of the seed,

A FOREST EXAMINER RUNNING A COMPASS LINE

the care and transplanting of the young trees until they are set out on the site of the future forest, forms a task of absorbing interest. Such work often requires a high degree of technical skill. It is likely to occupy a larger and larger share of the time and attention of the trained men of the Forest Service.

The Forest Assistant's or Examiner's knowledge of surveying makes it natural for him to take an important part in the laying out of new roads and trails in the forest, or in correcting the lines of old ones, and there is little work more immediately useful. The forest can be safeguarded effectively just in proportion to the ease with which all parts of it can be reached. Forest protection may be less technically interesting than other parts of the Forester's work, but nothing that he does is more important or pays larger dividends in future results.

THE TRAINING OF A FORESTER

In addition to his studies of the habits and reproduction of the different trees for working plans or timber sales, or simply to increase his knowledge of the forest, the Forest Examiner is often called upon to lay out sample plots for ascertaining the exact relation of each species to light, heat, and moisture, or for studying its rate of growth. He may find it necessary to determine the effect of the grazing of cattle or sheep on young growth of various species and of various ages, or to ascertain their relative resistance to fire. In general, what time he can spare from more pressing duties is very fully occupied with adding to his silvical knowledge by observation, with studies of injurious insects or fungi, of the reasons for the increase or decrease of valuable or worthless species of trees in the forest, the innumerable secondary effects of forest fires, the causes of the local distribution of trees,

60

or with some other of the thousand questions
which give a never-failing interest to work
in the woods.

The protection of a valuable kind of tree
often depends upon the ability to find a use
for, and therefore to remove, a less-valuable
species which is crowding it out, for as yet
the American Forester can do very little cutting or thinning that does not pay. Just so,
the protection of a given tract against fire
may depend upon the ability to use, and
therefore to remove, a part or the whole of
the dead and down timber which now makes
it a fire trap. For such reasons as these, the
uses of wood and the markets for its disposal form exceedingly important branches
of study for the Forest Examiner, who will
usually find that his duties require him to be
thoroughly familiar with them.

It is more and more common to find each
Forest Officer—Ranger, Forest Examiner,

THE TRAINING OF A FORESTER

or Supervisor—combining in himself the qualities and the knowledge required to fill any or all of the other positions. The professionally trained man who develops marked executive ability is likely to become a Supervisor, just as a Ranger, with the necessary training and experience, who may wish to devote himself to silvical investigations may be transferred to that work. The point is that each man has individual opportunity to establish and occupy the place for which he is best fitted.

The success of the technical Forester, like that of the Ranger, and indeed of nearly every Government Forest Officer, in whatever position or line of work, will very frequently depend on his good judgment and practical sense, the chief ingredient of which will always be his knowledge of local needs and conditions, and his sympathetic understanding of the local point of view. This does not mean that the local point of view is always to control. On the contrary, the Forest Officer must often decide against it in the interest of the welfare of the larger public. But the desires and demands of the users of the forest should always be given the fullest hearing and the most careful consideration. To this rule there is no exception whatsoever.

PERSONAL EQUIPMENT

FORESTRY differs from most professions in this, that it requires as much vigor of body as it does vigor of mind. The sort of man to which it appeals, and which it seeks, is the man with high powers of observation, who does not shrink from responsibility, and whose mental vigor is balanced by physical strength and hardiness. The man who takes up forestry should be little interested in his own personal comfort, and should have and conserve endurance enough to stand severe physical work accompanied by mental labor equally exhausting.

Foresters are still few in numbers, and the point of view which they represent, while it is making immense strides in public acceptance, is still far from general application. Therefore, Foresters are still missionaries in a very real sense, and since they are so few, it is of the utmost importance that they should stand closely together. Differences of opinion there must always be in all professions, but there is no other profession in which it is more important to keep these differences from working out into animosities or separations of any kind. We are fortunate above all in this, that American Foresters are united as probably the members of no other profession. This *esprit de corps* has given them their greatest power of achievement, and any man who proposes to enter the profession should do so with this fact clearly in mind.

The high standard which the profession of forestry, new in the United States, has already reached, its great power for usefulness to the Nation, now and hereafter, and the large responsibilities which fall so quickly on the men who are trained to accept it— all these things give to the profession a position and dignity which it should be the first care of every man who enters it to maintain or increase.

To stand well at graduation is or ought to be far less the object of a Forester's training than to stand well ten or twenty years after graduation. It is of the first importance that the training should be thorough and complete.

A friend of mine, John Muir, used to say that the best advice he could give young men was: "Take time to get rich." His idea of getting rich was to fill his mind and spirit full with observations of the nature he so deeply loved and so well understood; so that in his mind it was not money which makes riches, but life in the open and the seeing eye.

Next to those basic traits of personal character, without which no man is worth his salt, the Forester's most important quality is the power of observation, the power to note and understand, or seek to understand, what he sees in the forest. It is just as essential a part of the Forester's equipment to be able to see what is wrong with a piece of forest, and what is required for its improvement, as it is necessary for a physician to be able to diagnose a disease and to prescribe the remedy.

Silvics, which may be said to be the knowledge of how trees behave in health and disease toward each other, and toward light,

heat, moisture, and the soil, is the foundation
of forestry and the Forester's first task is to
bring himself to a high point of efficiency in
observing and interpreting these facts of the
forest, and to keep himself there. It should
be as hard work to walk through the forest,
and see what is there to be seen, as to wrestle
with the most difficult problem of mathematics. No man can be a good Forester
without that quality of observation and
understanding which the French call " the
forester's eye." It is not the only quality
required for success in forestry, but .it is
unquestionably the first.

Perhaps the second among the qualities
necessary for the Forester is common sense,
which most often simply means a sympathetic understanding of the circumstances
among which a man finds himself. The
American Forester must know the United
States and understand its people. Nothing

which affects the welfare of his country
should be indifferent to him. Forestry is a
form of practical statesmanship which
touches the national life at so many points
that no Forester can safely allow himself to
remain ignorant of the needs and purposes
of his fellow citizens, or to be out of touch
with the current questions of the day. The
best citizen makes the best Forester, and no
man can make a good Forester unless he is a
good citizen also.

The Forester can not succeed unless he
understands the problems and point of view
of his country, and that is the reason why
Foresters from other lands were not brought
into the United States in the early stages
of the forest movement. At that time
practically no American Foresters had yet
been trained, and the great need of the situation was for men to do the immediately
pressing work. Foresters from Germany,

THE TRAINING OF A FORESTER

France, Switzerland, and other countries could have been obtained in abundant numbers and at reasonable salaries. They were not invited to come because, however well trained in technical forestry, they could not have understood the habits of thought of our people. Therefore, in too many cases, they would have failed to establish the kind of practical understanding which a Forester must have with the men who use, or work in, his forest, if he is to succeed. It was wiser to wait until Americans could be trained, for the practising Forester must handle men as well as trees.

One of the most difficult things to do in any profession which involves drudgery (and I take it that no profession which does not involve drudgery is worth the attention of a man) is to look beyond the daily routine to the things which that routine is intended to assist in accomplishing. This is peculiarly true of forestry, in which, perhaps more than in any other profession, the long-distance, far-sighted attitude of mind is essential to success. The trees a Forester plants he himself will seldom live to harvest. Much of his thought about his forest must be in terms of centuries. The great object for which he is striving of necessity can not be fully accomplished during his lifetime. He must, therefore, accustom himself to look ahead, and to reap his personal satisfaction from the planned and orderly development of a scheme the perfect fruit of which he can never hope to see.

This is one of the strongest reasons why the Forester, whether in public or private employment, must always look upon himself as a public servant. It is of the first importance that he should accustom himself to think of the results of his work as affecting, not primarily himself, but others, always

THE TRAINING OF A FORESTER

including the general public. It is essential for a Forester to form the habit of looking far ahead, out of which grows a sound perspective and persistence in body and mind.

One of the greatest football players of our time makes the distinction between a player who is " quick " and a player who is " soon." In his description, the " quick " player is the man who waits until the last moment and then moves with nervous and desperate haste in the little time he has left. The man who is " soon," however, almost invariably arrives ahead of the man who is " quick," because he has thought out in advance exactly where he is going and how to get there, and when the moment comes he does not delay his start, makes no false motions, and thereby makes and keeps himself efficient. Forestry is preëminently a profession for the " soon " man, for it is the steady preparation long in advance, the well-thought-

71

out plan well stuck to, which in forestry brings success.

In my experience, men differ comparatively little in mere ability, in the quality of the mental machine.through which the spirit works. Nine times out of ten, it is not ability which brings success, but persistence and enthusiasm, which are usually, but not always, the same as vision and will. We all have ability enough to do the things which lie before us, but the man with the will to keep everlastingly at it, and the vision to realize the meaning and value of the results for which he is striving, is the man who wins in nearly every case. This is true in all human affairs, but it is peculiarly true of the Forester and his task, the end of which lies so far ahead.

In a class below me at Phillips-Exeter Academy was a boy who had just entered the school. His great ambition was to play

football, and he came to the practise day
after day. His abilities, however, were ap-
parently not on the same plane with his
ambitions, and his work was so ridiculously
poor that he became the laughing stock of
the whole school. That, however, troubled
him not at all. What held his mind was
football. Undiscouraged and undismayed,
he kept on playing football until in his last
year he became captain of the Exeter football team.

Every man of experience has known many
similar cases. It is clear, I think, that the
master qualities in achievement are neither
luck nor mere ability, but rather enthusiasm
and persistence, or vision and will.

In a peculiar sense the Forester depends
upon public opinion and public support for
the means of carrying on his work, and for
its final success. But the attention which
the public gives or can give to any particu-

lar subject varies, and of necessity must vary, from time to time. Under these circumstances, it is inevitable that the Forester must meet discouragements, checks, and delays, as well as periods of smooth sailing. He should expect them, and should be prepared to discount them when they come. When they do come, I know of no better way of reducing their bad effects than for a man to make allowance for his own state of mind. He who can stand off and look at himself impartially, realizing that he will not feel to-morrow as he feels to-day, has a powerful weapon against the temporary discouragements which are necessarily met in any work that is really worth while. Progress is always in spirals, and there is always a good time coming. There is nothing so fatal to good work as that flabby spirit under which some weak men try to hide their inefficiency—the spirit of " What's the use? "

74

THE TRAINING OF A FORESTER

It has been the experience of every Forester, as he goes about the country, to be told that a certain mountain is impassable, that a certain trail can not be travelled, that a certain stream can not be crossed, and to find that mountain, trail, and stream can all be passed with little serious difficulty by a man who is willing to try. Most things said to be impossible are so only in the mind of the man whose timidity or inertness keeps him from making the attempt. The whole story of the establishment and growth of the United States Forest Service is a story of the doing of things which the men who did them were warned in advance would be impossible. Usually the thing which "can't be done" is well worth trying.

Perhaps I ought to add that I am not urging the young Forester to disregard local public opinion without the best of reasons, or to rush his horse blindly into the ford of a swollen stream. Good sense is the first condition of success. I am merely saying that in ninety-nine cases out of a hundred, when a thing ought to be done it can be done, if the effort is made with that idea in mind.

All this is but one way of saying that the Forester should be his own severest taskmaster. The Forester must keep himself up to his own work. In no other profession, to my knowledge, is a man thrown so completely on his own responsibility. The Forester often leads an isolated life for weeks or months at a time, seeing the men under whom he works only at distant intervals. Because he is so much his own master, the responsibility which rests upon him is peculiarly his own, and must be met out of the resources within himself.

The training of a Forester should lead him to be practical in the right sense of that word, which emphatically is not the sense of

abandoning standards of work or conduct
in order to get immediate results. The
" practical " men with whom the Forester
must do his work—lumbermen, cattlemen,
sheepmen, settlers, forest users of all kinds
—are often by very much his superiors in
usable knowledge of the details of their
work. Their opinions are entitled to the
most complete hearing and respect. There
is no other class of men from whose advice
the Forester can so greatly profit if he
chooses to do so. He is superior to them,
if at all, only in his technical knowledge,
and in the broader point of view he has de-
rived from his professional training. It is
of the first importance that the young
Forester should know these men, should
learn to like and respect them, and that he
should get all the help he can from their
knowledge and practical experience. The
willingness to use the information and

assistance which such men were ready to give has more than once meant the difference between failure and success.

The young Forester, like other young men, is likely to be impatient. I do not blame him for it. Rightly directed, his impatience may become one of his best assets. But it will do no harm to remember, also, that the human race has reached its present degree of civilization and advancement only step by step, and that it seems likely to proceed in very much the same way hereafter. As a general rule, results slowly and painfully accomplished are lasting. The results to be achieved in forestry must be lasting if they are to be valuable.

In general, the men with whom the Forester deals can adopt, and in many cases, ought to adopt, a new point of view but slowly. To fall in love at first sight with theories or policies is as rare as the same experience is between persons. As a rule, an intellectual conviction, however well founded, must be followed by a period of incubation and growth before it can blossom into a definite principle of action, before the man who holds it is ready to work or fight in order to carry it out. There is a rate in the adoption of new ideas beyond which only the most unusual circumstances will induce men's minds to move. Forestry has gone ahead in the United States faster than it ever did in any other land. If it proceeds a little less rapidly, now that so much of the field has been won, there will be no reason for discouragement in that.

AS A SUBORDINATE OFFICER

Necessarily the young Forester will begin as a subordinate. How soon he will come to give orders of his own will depend on how well he executes the orders of his superior. In particular, it will depend on whether he requires to be coddled in doing his work, or whether he is willing and able to stand on his own feet. The man for whom every employer of men is searching, everywhere and always, is the man who will accept the responsibility for the work he has to do—who will not lean at every point upon his superior for additional instructions, advice, or encouragement.

There is no more valuable subordinate than the man to whom you can give a piece of work and then forget about it, in the confident expectation that the next time it is brought to your attention it will come in the form of a report that the thing has been done. When this master quality is joined to executive power, loyalty, and common sense, the result is a man whom you can trust. On the other hand, there is no greater nuisance to a man heavily burdened with the direction of affairs than the weak-backed assistant who is continually trying to get his chief to do his work for him, on the feeble plea that he thought the chief would like to decide this or that himself. The man to whom an executive is most grateful, the man whom he will work hardest and value most, is the man who accepts responsibility willingly, and is not continually under his feet.

AS A SUPERIOR OFFICER

The principles of effective administrative work have never, so far as I know, been adequately classified and defined. When they come to be stated one of the most important will be found to be the exact assignment of responsibility, so that whatever goes wrong the administrative head will know clearly and at once upon whom the responsibility falls. This is one of the reasons why, as a rule, boards and commissions are far less effective in getting things done than single men with clear-cut authority and equally clear-cut responsibility. Another principle, so well known that it has almost become a proverb, is to delegate everything you can, to do nothing that you can get someone else to do for you. But the wisdom of letting a good man alone is less commonly understood. It is sometimes as important for the superior officer not to worry his subordinate with useless orders as it is for the subordinate not to harass his superior with useless questions.

Let a good man alone. Give him his head. Nothing will hold him so rigidly to his work as the feeling that he is trusted. Lead your men in their work, and above all make of your organization not a monarchy, limited or unlimited, but a democracy, in which the responsibility of each man for a particular piece of work shall not only be defined but recognized, in which the credit for each man's work, so far as possible, shall be attached to his own name, in which the opinions and advice of your subordinates are often sought before decisions are made; in a word, a democracy in which each man feels a personal responsibility for the success of the whole enterprise.

The young Forester may be years removed from the chance to apply these principles in practice, but since no superior officer can put them into fruitful effect without the coöperation of his subordinates, it is well that they should be known at both ends of the line.

A PUBLIC SERVANT

I repeat that whether a Forester is engaged in private work or in public work, whether he is employed by a lumberman, an association of lumbermen, a fishing and shooting club, the owner of a great estate, or whether he is an officer of a State or of the Nation, by virtue of his profession he is a public servant. Because he deals with the forest, he has his hand upon the future welfare of his country. His point of view is that which must control its future welfare. He represents the planned and orderly development of its resources. He is the representative also of the forest school from which he graduates, and of his profession. Upon the standards which he helps to establish and maintain, the welfare of these, too, directly depends.

STATE FOREST WORK

THE work of the States in forestry is still in the pioneer stage, and the work of a State Forester must still bear largely on the creation of a right public sentiment in forest matters. In State forestry the need for agitation has by no means passed. It is often the duty of the State Forester to prepare or endeavor to secure the passage of good State forest laws, or to interpose against the enactment of bad laws. In particular, much of his time is likely to be given to legislation upon the subjects of forest fires and forest taxation. Upon the latter there is as yet no sound and effective public opinion in many parts of the United States, and legislatures and people still do not understand how powerful bad methods of forest taxation have been and still are in forcing the destructive cutting of timber by making it impossible to wait for the better methods of lumbering which accompany a better market. I have known the taxes on standing timber to equal six per cent. a year on the reasonable value of the stumpage.

THE TRAINING OF A FORESTER

Thirteen States have State Forests with a total area altogether of 3,600,000 acres. Of these New York has the largest area. Its State Forests cover 1,825,882 acres, partly in the Adirondacks and partly in the Catskills; Pennsylvania comes next with something over one million acres; and Wisconsin third, with about four hundred thousand acres.

Thirty-one States make appropriations for forest work. Excluding special appropriations for courses in forestry at universities, colleges, and schools, the total amount spent for this purpose is about $1,300,000. Pennsylvania has the largest appropriation, —three hundred and fifteen thousand dollars, in addition to which a special appropriation of two hundred and seventy-five thousand dollars was formerly devoted to checking the chestnut blight. New York comes second with one hundred and seventy-eight thousand dollars; Minnesota third with about one hundred and eighteen thousand dollars, and Michigan next with one hundred and five thousand dollars.

Thirty-two States have State forest officers, of whom nineteen are State Foresters by title, while the majority of the remainder perform duties of a very similar nature.

Twenty-one States are receiving assistance from the Federal Government under the Weeks law, which authorizes coöperation for fire protection, provided the State will furnish a sum equal to that allotted to it from the National fund, with a limit of ten thousand dollars to a single State.

For purposes of reforestation, ten States maintain forest nurseries. During the year 1912 they produced in round numbers twenty million young trees, of which fourteen million were distributed to the citizens of these ten States.

THE TRAINING OF A FORESTER

In some States the waterpower question falls within the sphere of the State Forester, as well as other similar Conservation matters, while it has usually been made his duty to assist private timberland owners in the handling of their holdings, whether these be the larger holdings of lumber companies or the farmers' woodlots. In many States the State Forester is made responsible for the enforcement of the State forest fire laws, and for the control and management of a body of State fire wardens, who may or may not be permanently employed in that work. The enforcement of laws which exempt timberlands or lands planted to timber from taxation, or limit the taxation upon them, are also usually under his supervision.

The work of forestry in the various States being on the whole much less advanced than it is in the Nation, the State Forester must still occupy himself largely with those preliminary phases of the work of forestry through which the National Forest Service has already passed. Much progress, however, is being made, and we may fairly count not only that State forest organizations will ultimately exist in every State, but that the State Foresters will exert a steadily increasing influence on forest perpetuation in the United States.

THE FOREST SERVICE IN WASHINGTON

A DESCRIPTION of what a Forester has to do which did not include the work of the Government Foresters at the National Capital would necessarily be incomplete. The following outline may, therefore, help to round out the picture.

The Washington headquarters of the Forest Service are directly in charge of the

Forester and his immediate assistants. The Forester has general supervision of the whole Service. It is he who, with the approval of the Secretary of Agriculture, determines the general policy which is to govern the Service in the very various and numerous matters with which it has to deal. He keeps his hand upon the whole machinery of the Service, holds it up to its work, and in general is responsible for supplying it with the right spirit and point of view, without which any kind of efficiency is impossible.

The Forester prepares the estimates, or annual budget, for the expenditures of the Service, and appears before Committees of Congress to explain the need for money, and otherwise to set forth or defend the work upon which the Service is engaged. His immediate subordinates spend a large part of their time in the field inspecting the work of the Service and keeping its tone high. Their reports to the Forester keep him thoroughly advised as to the situation on all the National Forests, so that he may wisely meet each question as it comes up, and adjust the regulations and routine business methods of the Service to the constantly changing needs of the people with whom it deals.

Being responsible for the personnel of the Forest Service, the Forester recommends to the Secretary of Agriculture, by whom the actual papers are issued, all appointments to it, as well as promotions, reductions, and dismissals. Under his immediate eye also is the very important and necessary work of making public the information collected by the Service for the use of the people. Since 1900, 534 publications of the Service have been issued, with a total circulation of 12,832,000 copies.

THE TRAINING OF A FORESTER

The publications of the United States Forest Service include by far the most and the best information upon the forests of this country which has until now been assembled and printed. Hence, the prospective student of forestry can do nothing better than to write to The Superintendent of Documents, Washington, D. C., for Price List 43, a catalogue of these publications, which are sent free to all applicants, and then to secure and study such of the bulletins and circulars as best meet his individual needs. If he looks forward to entering the United States Forest Service, he should not fail to get also the Use Book, the volume of directions and regulations in accordance with which the National Forests are protected, developed, and made available and useful to the people of the regions in which they lie.

The dendrological work of the Service, which has to do with forest distribution, the identification of tree species and other forest botanical work, is also under the immediate supervision of the Forester, and the Chief Lumberman reports directly to him.

In addition to the work which falls immediately under the eye of the Forester, and which used to, but does not now, include the legal work necessary to support and promote the operations of the Service, there are six principal parts, or branches, in the work of the Washington headquarters.

The first branch, that of Operation, has charge of the business administration both of the National Forests and of the other work of the Forest Service. Here the business methods which are necessary to keep the organization at a high state of efficiency are formulated, put in practice, and constantly revised, for it is only by such revision that they can be kept, as they are kept, at a level with the very best practice of the best modern business. There are very few Government bureaus of which this can be said.

The Branch of Operation is responsible for the adoption and enforcement of labor-saving devices in correspondence, in handling requisitions, and in the filing and care of papers generally, and for the supply of stationery, tools, and instruments, and the renting of quarters,—in a word, for the whole of the more or less routine transaction of business which is essential to keep so large an organization at the highest point of efficiency. It also has charge of accounts, whose value I need not describe further than to say that the Service has always owed a very large part of its safety against the bitter attacks of its enemies to the accuracy, completeness, and general high quality of its accounting system.

The office work needed in the mapping of

94

BRUSH PILING IN A NATIONAL FOREST TIMBER SALE

the National Forests, with all their resources, boundaries, and interior holdings, is in charge of the Branch of Operation. So is the immense amount of drafting which is necessary in the other work of the Service, and the photographic laboratory in which maps are reproduced and where permanent photographic records of the condition of the forest are made.

The second branch, that of Lands, has to do with the questions which arise from the use of the land in the National Forests for farming or ranching, mining, and a very wide variety of other purposes, and with the exceedingly numerous and intricate questions which arise because there are about 20,600,000 acres of land within the boundaries of the National Forests whose title has already passed from the Government. The boundaries of the National Forests also are constantly being examined to determine whether they include all the land, and only the land, rightly contained within them, and whether they should be extended or reduced.

The first permits for the use of water-power sites on Government land were issued by the Forest Service, and the policy which is now being adopted by the Interior Department and other Government organizations in their handling of waterpower questions was there first developed. These permits are prepared in the Branch of Lands. The first steps toward deterring men who attempt in defiance of the law to get possession of lands claimed to be agricultural or mineral within the National Forests are taken here, but the final decision on these points rests with the Department of the Interior. The examination of lands to determine whether they are agricultural in character, and therefore should be opened to settlement, is directed from this Branch.

THE TRAINING OF A FORESTER

The uses to which National Forest lands are put are almost unbelievably various. Barns, borrow pits, botanical gardens, cemeteries and churches, dairies and dipping vats, fox ranches and fish hatcheries, hotels, pastures, pipe lines, power sites, residences, sanitaria and school-houses, stores and tunnels, these and many others make up, with grazing and timber sales, the uses of the National Forests, for which already more than half a million permits have been issued. This work also falls to the Branch of Lands.

The third branch, that of Silviculture, is the most important of all. It has oversight of the practice of forestry on all the National Forests, and of all scientific forest studies in the National Forests and outside. It is here that the conditions in the contracts under which the larger timber sales are made are finally examined and approved, and here are found the inspectors whose duty it is not

only to see that the work is well done, but
to labor constantly for improvements in
methods as well as in results. Here centres
the preparation of forest working plans, and
the knowledge of lumber and the lumber
markets.

The Branch of Silviculture has charge also
of National coöperation for the advancement of forestry with the several States, and
in particular for fire protection under the
Weeks law. This form of coöperation has
made the knowledge and equipment of the
Forest Service available for the study of
State forest resources and forest problems,
and much of the progress in forestry made
by the States is directly due to it.

The fourth branch, that of Grazing, super-
vises the use of the National Forests for
pasture. Over the greater part of the West,
this was the first use to which the forests
were put, and an idea of its magnitude may

be gathered from the fact that every year
the National Forests supply feed for nearly
two million cattle and horses, and more than
fourteen million sheep.   It is no easy task to
permit all this live stock to utilize the forage
which the National Forests produce, and yet
do little or no harm to the young growth on
which the future of the forests depends.   To
exclude the grazing animals altogether is impossible and undesirable, for to do so would
ruin the leading industry in many portions
of the West.   Consequently, many of the
most difficult and perplexing questions in the
practical administration of the National Forests have occurred in the work of the Branch
of Grazing, and have there been solved, and
many of the most bitter attacks upon it have
there been met.

The fifth Branch is that of Research. As
a part of its numerous and varied duties it

brings together all that is known of the nature and growth of trees in this country, and to some extent in other countries also, conducts independent studies of the greatest value in developing better methods of securing the reproduction of important forest trees, and computes the enormous number of forest measurements dealing with the stand and the rate of growth of trees and forests that are turned in by the parties engaged in forest investigation in the field. Under the Branch of Research, various studies in forest distribution and in the structure of wood are carried on, and it includes the Library of the Forest Service, by far the most complete and effective forest library in the United States.

The branch of Research on another side is concerned with the whole question of the uses of wood and other materials produced by the forest. Its principal work is conducted through the Forest Products Laboratory, in coöperation with the University of Wisconsin at Madison. Here timber is tested to ascertain its strength, the products of wood distillation are investigated, wood pulp and paper studies of large reach are carried on, the methods of wood preservation and the results of applying them are in constant course of being examined, and the diseases of trees and of wood are studied in coöperation with the Bureau of Plant Industry of the United States Department of Agriculture. The consumption of wood, and the production of lumber and forest products, are also the subject of continuous investigation, and various necessary special studies are undertaken from time to time. A good example was the recent effort to find new uses and new markets for wood killed by the chestnut blight in the northeastern United States.

THE TRAINING OF A FORESTER

The sixth branch has to do with the study, selection, and acquisition of lands under the Weeks law, in accordance with which eleven million dollars was appropriated for the purchase of forest lands valuable for stream protection, with particular reference to the Southern Appalachians and the White Mountains of New England. The examination of the amount of merchantable timber on lands under consideration for purchase, the study of the character of the land and the forest, and the survey of the land keep a numerous body of young men very fully occupied. Their task is to see that none but the right land is recommended for acquisition by the Government, that the nature and value of the lands selected shall be most thoroughly known, and that the constant effort to make the Government pay unreasonable prices or purchase under unfavorable conditions shall as constantly be defeated.

The same branch takes charge of the lands as soon as they have been acquired.

The foregoing description of the work which is done in Washington by the Forest Service may help to make clear the great variety of tasks to which a Forester may be required to set his hand, and emphasizes the need of a broad training not strictly confined to purely technical lines. It would be defective as a description, however, and would fail to show the spirit in which the work is done, if no mention were made of the Service Meeting, at which the responsible heads of each branch and of the work of the Forester's office meet once a week to discuss every problem which confronts the Service and every phase of its work. This meeting is the centre where all parts of the work of the Service come together and arrange their mutual coöperation, and it is also the spring from which the essential democracy of the organization takes its rise. The Service Meeting is the best thing in the Forest Service, and that is saying a great deal.

It must not be imagined that the maintenance of Forest Service headquarters in Washington indicates that the actual business of handling the National Forests is carried on at long range. In order to avoid any such possibility seven District offices were organized. These are situated at Missoula, Denver, Albuquerque, Portland, Ogden, San Francisco, and Washington. Each of the District offices is in charge of a District Forester, who directs the practical carrying out of the policies finally determined upon in Washington, after consultation with the men in the field. The execution of all the work, the larger features of which the Washington office decides and directs (and the details of which it inspects), is the task of the District Forester. The

104

FOREST RANGERS GETTING INSTRUCTION IN METHODS OF WORK FROM A DISTRICT FOREST OFFICER

THE TRAINING OF A FORESTER

District Forester's office is necessarily organized much on the same general lines as the Washington headquarters. Thus, the subjects of accounts, operation, silviculture, grazing, lands, and forest research are all represented in the District offices. In addition, a legal officer is necessarily attached to each District office, and each District Forester has in his District one or more forest experiment stations, employed mainly in studying questions of growth and reproduction; and three forest insect field stations, maintained for coöperation by the Bureau of Entomology, are divided among the Districts.

While the work of the Washington office is mainly that of guiding the work of the National Forests along broad general lines, through instructions to the District Foresters, the office of each District Forester deals directly with the Forest Supervisors, and so with the handling of the National Forests.

THE TRAINING OF A FORESTER

A multitude of questions which the Supervisors can not answer are decided in the District office instead, as was formerly the case, of being forwarded to Washington for disposal there, with the consequent aggravating and needless delay. The establishment of the District offices has made the handling of the National Forests far less complicated and far more prompt, and has brought it far closer than ever before to the actual users, —that is, has made it far more quickly and accurately responsive to their needs.

PRIVATE FORESTRY

As yet, the practice of forestry by private owners, except for fire protection, has made but little progress in the United States, although without doubt it will be widely extended during the next ten or fifteen years. The concentration of timberland ownership

106

in the United States has put a few men in control of vast areas of forest. Many of them are anxious to prevent forest destruction, so far as that may be practicable without interfering with their profits, and for that purpose Foresters are beginning to be employed. Until now the principal tasks of Foresters employed by lumbermen have been the measurement of the amount of lumber in the standing crop of trees, and the protection of forest lands from fire. Here and there the practice of a certain amount of forestry has been added, but this part of the work of the private Forester employed by lumbermen has not been important. It is likely, however, to increase with some rapidity before long. In the meantime, the private Forester must usually be willing to accept a good many limitations on the technical side of his work.

It is essential for the Forester thus employed to have or promptly to acquire a knowledge of practical lumbering, that is, of logging, milling, and markets, and for the forest student who expects to enter this work to give special attention to these subjects.

Already about 200 graduates of forest schools are in private employ, a considerable proportion of which number are employed by large lumbermen.

The time is undoubtedly coming, and I hope it may come soon, when forest destruction will be legally recognized as hostile to the public welfare, and when lumbermen will be compelled by law to handle their forests so as to insure the reproduction of them under reasonable conditions and within a reasonable time. The idea is neither tyrannical nor new. In democratic Switzerland, private owners of timberland are restrained by law from destroying the forests upon which the welfare of that mountain region so largely depends, and if they disobey, their forest lands are replanted by the Government at the owners' expense.

Another opening for Foresters in the employ of lumbermen is through the forest fire protective associations. Of these, two stand out most conspicuously at the present time, one the Western Forestry and Conservation Association, the other the Oregon Forest Fire Association. Each has as its executive officer a trained Forester whose knowledge of the woods not only makes him exceedingly useful to his employers, but also, when combined with the Forester's point of view, enables him to be of great value in protecting the general interest in the forest.

The object and methods of one of the associations is described by its Secretary as follows:

THE TRAINING OF A FORESTER

" A field hitherto narrow but continually broadening, and offering much opportunity for those with peculiar qualifications, is the management of the coöperative forest work carried on by timber owners in many localities, often jointly with State and Government. This movement originated in the Pacific Northwest, where it still has the highest development, but is extending to the Lake States, New England, and Canada.

" As a rule the primary object of these coöperative associations is fire prevention and their local managers must have demonstrated ability to organize effective patrol systems, build telephone lines, apply every ingenuity to supplying and equipping their forces, and, above all, to handle men in emergencies. But in most cases the association of forest owners to this end has led also to progress in many other matters inseparable from improvement, such as study of reforestation possibilities, forest legislation, educating lumberman and public in forest preservation, and the extension of coöperation in all these as well as in fire prevention from private to State and federal agencies.

" The development of such activities is already employing several highly paid men who can command the confidence, not only of forest owners, but also of the public and of public officials. Advisers in legislative as well as technical forestry matters and particularly proficient in all that pertains to forest protection, their usefulness lies as much outside their own association as within them, and to be successful they must be skilful organizers and campaigners. It is these men who have developed to its highest extent the adaptation to forestry propaganda of modern publicity and advertising methods.

" As a rule, however, these may be described as graduate positions, filled by men of experience and acquaintance with the several agencies involved, rather than by newly fledged Foresters. A practical knowledge of protection problems is essential."

Forestry associations offer a different, but often a most fascinating field, of work for the trained Forester. There are at present 39 such associations. The work which they offer has much in common with the duties of a State Forester.

Fish and game associations are beginning to employ Foresters, realizing that the wise handling of the forests may well go hand in hand with the care of the game and fish which the forest shelters and protects. Eventually nearly all such associations which control any considerable body of land in timbered regions may be expected to utilize the services of trained Foresters of their own.

THE TRAINING OF A FORESTER

In addition to the work for lumbermen and for associations of various kinds, land owners in considerable variety have begun to employ Foresters. Among these are coal and coke companies, iron companies, wood pulp and paper companies which are beginning to look after their supply of timber; powder, arms, and ammunition companies, hydraulic and water companies; a great corporation engaged in the manufacture of matches; and a number of railroads, including the Delaware and Hudson, the Illinois Central, and the Pennsylvania. In addition to the need for cross ties, railroads are among the largest consumers of lumber. The Foresters who work for them are largely occupied with growing the wood supplies which the railroads need, and nursery practice often occupies a very large share of their attention.

THE TRAINING OF A FORESTER

FOREST SCHOOLS

SINCE the first one was founded in 1898, the number of forest schools in the United States has increased so rapidly as to create a demand for forest instructors which it has been exceedingly difficult to fill. Indeed, the increase in secondary forest schools, or schools not of the first grade, has doubtless been more rapid than the welfare of the profession or the sound practice of forestry required, and the brisk demand for teachers has led some men to take up the task of instruction who were not well fitted for it.

There are in this country to-day 23 forest schools which prepare men for the practice of forestry as a profession, and 51 schools which devote themselves to general instruction in forestry or to courses for Forest Rangers and Forest Guards. The approximate number of teachers in all forest schools is at present 110, and this number will doubtless be still further increased by the addition of new forest schools or the expansion of old ones, while a certain number of places will be made vacant by the retirement of men who find themselves better fitted for other lines of work.

The teaching staff at three of the principal forest schools of the country was as follows:

At School A, 5 men give their whole time to forest instruction, and 14 give courses in the forest school.

Schools B and C have each 4 men who give their whole time to the work; and 4 and 20 respectively who give lectures or individual courses.

In addition to the work for lumbermen, associations, railroads, and others just mentioned, an increasing number of Foresters are required to care for the forests on large landed estates in different parts of the country. Work of this kind is at present restricted almost entirely to the East, and especially to New England, where several firms of consulting Foresters give to it the larger portion of their time. Some of the men thus employed are as fully occupied with the tasks of the professional Forester as any of the men in the Government service, while others give a part of their attention to the general management of the property, or to the protection and propagation of game and fish.

THE OPPORTUNITY

GOVERNMENT SERVICE

THERE is no more useful profession than forestry. The opportunity to make himself count in affairs of public importance comes earlier and more certainly to the Forester than to the member of any other profession. The first and most valuable, therefore, of the incentives which lead the Forester to his choice is the chance to make himself of use to his country and to his generation.

But if this is the first matter to be considered in deciding upon a profession, it is by no means the last, and the practical considerations of a fair return for good work, bread and butter for a man and his family, the certainty or uncertainty of employment, —such questions as these must have their full share of attention.

There are in the United States Forest Service 664 Forest Guards, 1091 Forest Rangers, 230 Supervisors and Deputy Supervisors, and 48 Forest Assistants and 146 Forest Examiners, who, as already explained, are the technical men in charge of practical forestry on the National Forests. The seven District offices together include in their membership about 50 professional Foresters, and about 40 more are attached to the headquarters at Washington, so that allowing for duplications there are about 350 trained Foresters in the United States Forest Service.

The number of new appointments to the Forest Service in the different permanent grades varies from year to year but may be said to be approximately as follows: Rangers, 110 new appointments; Forest Assistants, 10; other technical positions, 25. All appointments as Supervisors are by promotion from the lists of Forest Rangers or Forest Examiners.

The yearly pay of the Forest Guard, who, like the Ranger, must be a citizen of the State in which his work lies, is from $540 to $900. Forest Rangers, who enter the Service through Civil Service examination, receive from $600 to $1500 per annum.

THE TRAINING OF A FORESTER

Forest Supervisors, practically all of whom are men of long experience in forest work, receive from $1600 to $2800 per annum. Forest Assistants enter the Forest Service through Civil Service examination at a salary of $1100 per annum, and are promoted to a maximum salary of $2400 per annum, as Forest Examiners. Professional Foresters at work in the District offices are recruited mainly from among the Forest Assistants and Examiners. They receive from $1100 to $3200 yearly. The technical men in charge at Washington get from $1100 to $5000 per annum, which last is the pay of the Forester, at the head of the Service.

STATE SERVICE

The pay of the State Foresters, or other trained Foresters in charge of State work, ranges from $2000 to $5000, and that of their technical assistants from $1000 to $2500. Out of the total number, only 3 are directly in charge of their own work, responsible only to the Governor and the Legislature, while 26 act as subordinates for State forest commissions or commissioners, who in the majority of cases are political appointees. In striking contrast with the United States Forest Service, politics has so far been a dangerous, if not a dominating, influence in the forest work of most of the States which have undertaken it.

Like the National Forests, the State Forests already in existence will create an increasing demand for the service of technical Foresters. Indeed, as similar forests are acquired by most of the States which are now without them, as undoubtedly they will be, the extent of the opportunity for professionally trained Foresters in State work is certain to grow.

THE TRAINING OF A FORESTER

At present, the demand for Foresters in private work is far less pressing and the opening is far less attractive than it will be in the not distant future. The number of men that will be required for this work will depend on the development of legislation as well as upon the desire of the private owners, lumbermen and others, to protect and improve their property. The time is coming, and coming before long, when all private owners of forests in the mountains, or on steep slopes elsewhere, will be required by law to provide for their protection and reproduction. When that time arrives, the demand for Foresters in private work will increase to very large dimensions, and will probably do so far more rapidly than Foresters can be trained to supply it.

The pay of Foresters in private work, whether in the employ of lumbermen, railroads, shooting and fishing clubs, the proprietors of large private estates, or other forest owners, has so far been somewhat better than that for similar services in Government employ. This money difference in favor of private employment is, in my judgment, likely to continue, and eventually the pay of consulting Foresters of established reputation employed in passing upon the value of forests offered as security for investments, or in estimating the standing timber for purchasers or sellers, or in other professional work of large business importance, will certainly reach very satisfactory figures.

TEACHING

Approximately 110 Foresters are engaged in teaching in the United States today. Their pay varies from about $1000 to about $3000, and is likely to increase rather more rapidly than that of other professional teachers, since less of them are available. It is not likely, however, that the number of openings in teaching forestry will be large within the next ten years.

TRAINING

THE length of time which his training is to take and the particular courses of instruction which he shall pursue are to the young man contemplating the study of forestry matters of the first importance. The first thing to insist on in that connection is that the training must be thorough. It is natural that a young man should be eager to begin his life work and therefore somewhat impatient of the long grind of a thorough schooling. But however natural, it is not the part of wisdom to cut short the time of preparation. When the serious work of the trained Forester begins later on, there will be little or no time to fill the gaps left at school, and the earnest desire of the young Forester will be that he had spent more time in his preparation rather than less. In this matter I speak as one who has gathered a conviction from personal experience, and believes he knows.

It would be useless to attempt to strike an average of the work prescribed and the courses given at the various forest schools. I shall describe, therefore, not an average system of instruction but one which, in the judgment of men entitled to an opinion, and in my own judgment, is sound, practical, and effective.

Forest schools may roughly be divided between those which do not prepare men for professional work in forestry, and those which do. The latter may be divided again into undergraduate schools and graduate schools. Most of the former offer a four-year undergraduate course, and their students receive their degrees at the same time as other members of the University who entered at the same time with them. The graduate schools require a college degree, or its equivalent in certain subjects, before they will receive a student. The men who have completed their courses have usually, therefore, pursued more extensive and more advanced studies in forestry, are better trained, and are themselves older and more ready to accept the responsibilities which forestry brings upon them. For these reasons, the graduate school training is by far the more desirable, in my opinion.

The subjects required for entrance to a graduate forest school should include at least one full year in college botany, covering the general morphology, histology, and physiology of plants, one course each in geology, physics, inorganic chemistry, zoölogy, and economics, with mathematics through trigonometry, and a reading knowledge of French or German. Some acquaintance with mechanical drawing is also desirable but not absolutely necessary. Other courses which are extremely desirable, if not altogether essential, are mineralogy, meteorology, mechanics, physical geography, organic chemistry, and possibly calculus, which may be of use in timber physics.

One or two forest schools begin their course of training for the first year in July instead of in October, in order to give their students some acquaintance with the woods from the Forester's standpoint before the more formal courses begin. The result of this plan is to give increased vividness and reality to all the courses which follow the work in the woods, to make clear the application of what is taught, and so to add greatly to the efficiency of the teaching.

In addition to this preliminary touch with the woods, any wise plan of teaching will include many forest excursions and much practical field work as vitally important parts of the instruction. This outdoor work should occur throughout the whole course, winter and summer, and in addition, the last term of the senior year may well be spent wholly in the woods, where the students can be trained in the management of logging operations and milling, and can get their final practice work in surveying and map-making, in preparing forest working plans, estimating timber, laying out roads and trails, making plans for lumber operations, and other similar practical work. Several of the best forest schools have adopted this plan.

The regular courses of a graduate forest school usually cover a period of two years. They should fit a student for nearly every phase of professional work in forestry, and should give him a sound preparation not merely for practical work in the woods, but also for the broader work of forest organization in the Government Service in the United States and in the Philippines, and in the service of the States; for handling large tracts of private forest lands; for expert work in the employ of lumbermen and other forest owners; for public speaking and writing; for teaching; and for scientific research.

Every well equipped forest school will have a working library of books, pamphlets, and lumber journals published here and abroad, an herbarium at least of native trees and shrubs and of the more important forest herbs, together with a collection of forest tree fruits and seeds, and specimens of domestic and foreign timbers. Exhibits showing the uses of woods and the various forms of tools used in lumbering, as well as the apparatus for laboratory work and surveying, and forest instruments for work in the field, are often of great value to the student.

What should a young man learn at a forest school? Doubtless there will be some variation of opinion as to the exact course of study which will best fit him for the work of a Forester in the United States. The following list expresses the best judgment on the subject I have been able to form:

DENDROLOGY:

The first step in forestry is to become acquainted with the various kinds of trees. The coming Forester must learn to identify the woody plants of the United States, both in summer and in winter. He must understand their shapes and outward structures, and where they are found, and he must begin his knowledge of the individual habits of

9 129

growth and life which distinguish the trees
which are important in forestry.

Forest Physiography:

Trees grow in the soil. It is important to
know something of the origin of soils and
their properties and values, and of the
principal soil types, with special reference
to their effect upon plant distribution and
welfare. The origin, nature, value, and conservation of humus, that most essential ingredient of the forest floor; the field methods
of mapping soil types; the rock types most
important in their relation to soils, how they
are made up, how they make soil, and where
they occur—something should be learned of
all this. Finally, under this head, the student ought to get a usable knowledge of the
physiographic regions of the United States,
their boundaries, geologic structure, topog-
raphy, drainage, and soils,—all this natu-

rally with special reference to the relation between these basic facts and the forest.

SILVICULTURE:

Silviculture is the art of caring for forests, and therefore the backbone of forestry. It is based upon Silvics, which is the knowledge of the habits or behavior of trees in their relations to light, heat, and moisture, to the air and soil, and to each other. It is the facts embraced in Silvics which explain the composition, character, and form of the forest; the success or failure of tree species in competition with each other; the distribution of trees and of forests; the development of each tree in height, diameter, and volume; its form and length of life; the methods of its reproduction; and the effect of all these upon the nature and the evolution of the city of trees, and upon forest types and their life histories.

131

THE TRAINING OF A FORESTER

This is knowledge the Forester can not do without. Silvics is the foundation of his professional capacity, and as a student he can better afford to scamp any part of his training rather than this. A man may be a poor Forester who knows Silvics, but no man can be a good Forester who does not.

The practice of Silviculture has to do with the treatment of woodlands. The forest student must learn the different methods of reproducing forests by different methods of cutting them down, and the application of these methods in different American forest regions. There are also many methods of cutting for the improvement of the character and growth of forests, as well as for utilizing material that otherwise would go to waste, before the final reproduction cuttings can be made. The ways in which forests need protection are equally numerous, and of these by far the most important in our country have to do with methods of preventing or extinguishing forest fires.

Well managed forests are handled under working plans based on the silvical character and silvicultural needs of the forest, as well as upon the purpose set by the owner as the object of management, which is often closely related to questions of forest finance. The student should ground himself thoroughly in the making of silvicultural working plans, and the more practice in making them he can get, the better. So, too, with the marking of trees in reproduction and improvement cuttings under as many different kinds of forest conditions as may be possible.

The artificial reproduction of forests is likely to occupy far more of the Forester's attention in the future than it has in the past. Hence the collection of tree seeds, their fertility and vitality as affecting their handling, the best methods of seeding and planting, and the lessons of past failures and successes, with the whole subject of nursery work and the care of young plantations, must by no means be overlooked.

Much incidental information on the subject of forest protection will come to the student in the course of his studies, but special attention should be given to learning which of the species of forest insects are most injurious to forest vegetation, how their attacks are made, how they may be discovered, and the best ways by which such attacks can be mitigated or controlled. So also the diseases of timber trees will repay hard study. The principal fungi which causes such diseases should be known, how they attack the trees, and what are the remedies, as well as (although this is far less important) the way to treat tree wounds and the correct methods of pruning.

THE TRAINING OF A FORESTER

FOREST ECONOMICS:

Forest Economics is a large subject. It deals with the productive value of forests to their owners, and with the larger question of their place in the economy of the Nation. It considers their use as conservers of the soil and the streams; their effect on climate, locally, as in the case of windbrakes, and on a larger scale; and their contribution to the public welfare as recreation grounds and game refuges. It includes a knowledge of wastes from which the forests suffer, and the consequent loss to industry and to the public, and in this it does not omit the effects of forest fires. Statistics of forest consumption; the relation of the forest to railroads, mines, and other wood-using industries; its effect upon agriculture, stock raising, and manufacturing industries; and its effect upon the use of the streams for navigation, power, irrigation, and domestic water sup-

ply; all these are important. The student
should consider also the forest resources of
the United States, their present condition,
and the needs they must be fitted to supply.

FOREST ENGINEERING:

Forest engineering is steadily becoming
more and more necessary to the Forester.
He must have a working knowledge of the
use of surveying instruments; the making
of topographic surveys; the office work required of an engineer; the making of topographic maps; the location of trails, roads,
and railroads; and the construction of
bridges, telephone lines, cabins, and fences,
together with logging railroads, slides, dams,
and flumes.

FOREST MENSURATION:

Forest mensuration, the art of measur-
ing the contents and growth of trees and
forest stands, is of fundamental importance.

136

FOREST SERVICE MEN MAKING FOREST MEASUREMENTS IN THE
MISSOURI SWAMPS

THE TRAINING OF A FORESTER

The principles and methods of timber estimating, the actual measurement of standing timber, log rules, the making of stem analyses to show the increase of a tree in diameter, height, and volume, the construction of tables of current and mean annual growth per acre and per tree, and the methods of using the information thus formulated,—all these are necessarily of keen interest to the man who later on will have to apply his knowledge in the practical management of woods.

FOREST MANAGEMENT:

Forest management is concerned with the principles involved in planning the handling of forests. Questions of the valuation of forests form a most essential part of it,— such questions as the cost of growing timber crops, the value of land for that purpose, the value of young timber, the valuation of

137

damage to the forest, and the legal status of the damage and the remedy.

Business principles are as necessary in the management of forests as in the management of mills or farms. These business principles work out in different forms of forest policy adapted to the needs of different kinds of owners, such as lumbermen and the Government. What the young Forester has learned about growth and yield, about timber estimates and forest statistics, and many other matters, all finds its application in forest management. He must also consider the methods and principles for regulating the cut of timber, or for securing sustained annual yields. All this forms the basis for the preparation of working plans for the utilization of forests under American economic and silvicultural conditions, not only without injury, but with benefit, to their continued productiveness.

THE TRAINING OF A FORESTER

The subjects of forest surveying and working plans are intimately related. Maps are indispensable in the practical work of making a forest working plan. Topographic mapping, timber estimating, forest description, and the location of logging roads, trails, and fire lines, together with Silvics and a knowledge of growth and yield—these and many other subjects enter into the making of a practical working plan to harvest a forest crop and secure a second growth of timber. The student should get all the practice he can in marking timber for cutting under such a plan.

The young Forester must make himself familiar with the administration of the National Forests. He must know how the business of the forest is handled, how it is protected against fire, how the timber is sold, how claims and entries are dealt with under the public land laws, how land in the

National Forests is used to make homes, how trespass is controlled, how the livestock industry on the National Forests is fostered and regulated, and how the extremely valuable watersheds they contain are safeguarded and improved.

THE PRACTICE OF FORESTRY:

The practice of forestry is necessarily different in different kinds of forests and under different economic conditions. All that the Forester knows must here be applied, and applied in workable fashion, not only to the forest, but to the men who use the forest. This is peculiarly true of the practice of forestry in National and State Forests everywhere.

FOREST PRODUCTS:

Under this general subject, the forest student must acquaint himself, through the

140

microscope, with the minute anatomy of the woody stem of coniferous and broadleaf trees, and the occurrence, form, structure, and variability of the elements which make it up. He should become familiar with the methods of classifying the economic woods of the United States, both under the microscope and with the unassisted eye, and for this purpose should know something of their color, gloss, grain, density, odor, and resonance both as aids to identification and as to their importance in giving value to the wood; the defects of timber; its moisture content, density, shrinking, checking, warping; and the effect of all these upon its uses.

The chemical composition of wood and of minor forest products, such as tannins and dye stuffs, is important; the properties governing the fuel value and the other values of wood must be studied, as well as the methods of using these properties in the making of charcoal and wood pulp, in wood distillation, the turpentine industry, in tanning and dyeing, and in other industries.

A field of great importance is the relation between the physical structure and the mechanical properties of wood. A student should inform himself concerning the standard methods of testing the properties of structural timber, by bending, compression, shearing, torsion, impact, and the hardness and tension tests, with their relation to heat and moisture, and the methods of seasoning, the use of preservatives, and the effect of the rate of application of the load.

Woods vary as to their durability. It is important, therefore, to know about the causes of decay, the decay-resisting power of various woods, the relation of moisture content to durability, why the seasoning of wood is effective, the theory and the commercial methods of wood preservation, and its relation to the timber supply.

LUMBERING:

Lumbering the Forester should know more than a little about, as how to organize lumber operations, the equipment and management of logging and milling in various forest regions, the manufacture, seasoning, and grading of the rough and finished lumber, cost keeping in a lumber business, methods of sale, market requirements at home and abroad, prices, the relation of the lumber tariff to forestry, lumber associations, timber bonds, and insurance. The practical construction of logging equipment, such as aerial tramways, log slides, dams, and flumes, is of peculiar importance, and so are the conditions and changes of the lumber market.

Experience on the land of some operating lumber company is of great value. It should include a study of logging methods, log scaling, waste in logging, the equipment and handling of the mill, the sawing and care of rough and finished lumber, its grading, and so far as possible an acquaintance with wood working plants of various kinds, and with the operations of turpentine orcharding. Studies along these lines may with advantage be almost indefinitely extended to include, for example the utilization of steam machinery for logging, the improvement of streams for driving logs, and other similar questions.

FOREST LAW:

The Forester must have at least a slight acquaintance with forest law, both State and National. It is important to know something of the general principles of classifying the public lands, of State laws for fire protection, the development of forest policies in the various States as legally expressed, and the important laws which govern the creation and management of State forest reserves.

Forest taxation, State and local, which has, when excessive, so much to do with hastening forest destruction, is one of the most important questions which can engage the attention of the Forester.

Under the subject of Federal Forest Law, it is not sufficient for the student to acquaint himself with those laws alone which govern the forests. He must also have some knowledge of the creation of a forest policy out of the public land policy of the United States, some acquaintance with the public land laws. A good working knowledge of the laws and regulations governing the National Forests is indispensable, and the student should at least know where to find

10 145

the more important court decisions by which they are interpreted.

FOREST HISTORY:

The history of forestry in Europe has a certain importance in throwing light on our own forest history and its probable development, and this is especially true of the history of the administration of Government forest lands and of education in forestry.

The history of forestry in the United States, however, is far more important. The Forester must know the story of the growth and change of National Forest organizations, the Forest Officers and their duties, the cost, size, and effectiveness of the Government Forest Service at different times, the Civil Service regulations under which it is recruited, and other similar matters. It is important likewise for him to become thoroughly saturated with an intimate knowledge of the development of forestry in public opinion in the United States, its extension to the other natural resources through the conservation policy, and the relation of the Forester's point of view thus expressed to the present welfare and future success of the Nation.

It is not always possible for the forest student to become a woodsman before entering his profession, but it is most desirable. A Forester must be able to travel the forest alone by day and by night, he should be a good fisherman and a good hunter (which is far more important than to be a good shot), and deeply interested in both fish and game. The better horseman he is the better Forester he will be, and especially if he can pack and handle pack horses in the woods. So that whether the young Forester begins with a practical knowledge of woodcraft or not, he must not fail to acquire or improve it, for without it he will endanger the whole success of his career.

Some knowledge of first aid to the injured is likely to be of great and sudden value to a man so much of whose life must be spent in the woods, at a distance from medical aid. The time spent in getting information on this subject will be anything but wasted.

ENGLISH:

The ability to write and to speak good, plain, understandable English is a prime requisite in the Forester's training. It is a part of education frequently neglected, especially by those in engineering or scientific pursuits; yet its importance for the Forester is very large. As already pointed out, the Forester is on the firing line of the conservation movement; he is pioneering in a new profession. For this reason he will often need to explain his stand and convert others

148

to his beliefs. In addition, he must make available to others the results he secures from the study of new facts. A usable command of his own language will stand him in good stead, whether he needs to talk face to face with another man, or from a platform to a concourse of people, or to put into readable printed form the results of his observations or his thinking.

When the young Forester has completed the courses of his school training in America, the question may be raised whether he should supplement his training by study abroad. I am strongly of opinion that he should do so if he can. Study abroad is not indispensable for the American Forester, but it can do him nothing but good to see in practical operation the methods of forestry which have resulted from the long experience of other lands, and especially to become familiar with the effect of sound forestry on the forest.

SOME FACTS ABOUT OUR FORESTS

The forests of the United States originally covered an area of some 800,000,000 acres, but are now reduced to 550,000,000 acres, of which about 190,000,000 acres are in farm woodlots, and 360,000,000 acres in larger bodies of forest. These forests are naturally divided into the following regions:

The Northern Forest, which extends from Maine to northern Georgia along the Appalachian Mountains, and spreads westward over the region of the Great Lakes. The white, red, and jack pines, firs, spruces, and the beech, birches, and maples are its characteristic trees.

The Southern Forest, which follows the coast from southern New Jersey to Texas with an extension northward over Arkansas into southern Missouri. The yellow pines, the oaks, hickories, and the cypress are characteristic of this region.

The Central Forest, lying mainly between the Northern and the Southern Forests, but extending in a narrow belt from Massachusetts along the eastern border of the Appalachian Mountains to northern Georgia and Alabama. Thence it spreads north and west through the timbered bottoms of the Ohio and the Mississippi, until it dies out along the rivers of the great plains at about the one-hundredth meridian. The chief trees of this Central Forest are the oaks, hickories, and the chestnut, walnut, yellow poplar, cherry, and cottonwood.

The Rocky Mountain Forest covers the higher lands of the mountainous West from Mexico to the Canadian line. Its characteristic trees are the yellow pine, the Douglas fir, with spruce, firs, and the aspen.

The Pacific Coast Forest, except for an

isolated body along the Continental Divide
in Idaho, Montana, and Washington, follows
the coast and the Cascade and Sierra Mountains from Canada to Mexico. It contains
the most magnificent coniferous timberlands
of the world. Among its characteristic trees
are the Douglas fir, the sugar pine, many
firs and spruces, larches, cedars, yellow and
white pine, with the redwoods and the big
trees.

Southern Florida contains a small area of
sub-tropical forest, which has, however, little
more than botanical interest.

The total amount of saw timber in the
United States was once upwards of 5000
billion feet. It has been reduced nearly
one-half, so that to-day we have about 2800
billion board feet left. Fire, waste, and lumbering are each about equally responsible
for this reduction.

Of the lumber which our forests still contain, nearly three-quarters—or more than 2000 billion feet—is privately owned.

The National Forests contain a little less than one-quarter—21 per cent.—or nearly 600 billion board feet.

About 5 per cent.—or 130 billion board feet—is owned by the Government outside the National Forests, by the States, and by municipalities.

More than one-half of the country's timber is in the Pacific Northwest.

More than one-fourth is in the Southern pine region.

Not quite 4 per cent. (110 billion feet) is in the Lake States.

About 9 per cent. (242 billion feet) is in the Northeastern States.

Our supply of standing timber is yearly reduced by the following amounts:

About 40 billion feet of saw timber, 90 million cords of firewood, 445 million board feet of veneer, 150 million ties, nearly 1700 million staves, over 135 million sets of heading, over 350 million barrel hoops, over 3,300,000 cords of native pulpwood, 170 million cubic feet of round mine timbers, nearly 1,500,000 cords of wood for distillation, over 140,000 cords for excelsior, and nearly 3,500,000 telegraph and telephone poles.

Nearly half of our annual cut of saw timber comes from the southern pine region. The Lake States produce about one-sixth, and the Pacific Northwest about one-seventh.

The State which produces the most lumber is Washington, followed by Louisiana, Mississippi, North Carolina, Texas, Arkansas, and Oregon in the order named.

Oregon has more standing timber than any other State—545 billion board feet, or about one-fifth of all the standing timber in the United States.

THE TRAINING OF A FORESTER

The annual growth of well-managed forests in such a region as the United States may be taken as fifty cubic feet per acre per annum. Actually, we are growing about twelve cubic feet per acre per annum.

Our timber is being used up nearly three times faster than it is growing.

No other Nation has so large a consumption of timber per capita as the United States. We use about 250 cubic feet of wood per year for every man, woman, and child in the country.

Our present forest area, assuming that we have a population of 100,000,000, is about five and one-half acres per person. Clearing land for farms, and other causes, will doubtless reduce our forest area to 450,000,-000 acres. When our population reaches 150,000,000, and our forest area the amount just given, we shall have only three acres for each inhabitant, or at our present rate of forest growth, about thirty-six cubic feet per person where we now use 250.

Our individual consumption could easily be reduced to 150 or even 100 cubic feet per inhabitant per year without hardship by the use of substitutes and the elimination of waste.

We use now, on the average, only about one-half of the total volume of every tree. The rest is wasted, or left in the woods.

Forest fires still destroy every year about twelve billion board feet of timber, or more than one-fourth of the amount sawed in our mills.

The product of the lumber industry in 1909 was valued by the Census at $1,156,-000,000, which in amount was exceeded among the manufacturing industries only by meats and metals. In the number of men employed (over 900,000) the lumber industry comes first.

There are two and a third billion dollars

invested in the lumber industry, whose 49,000 mills are capable of cutting 117 billion feet per year, an amount more than two and one-half times greater than the largest they have ever produced, which was 46 billion feet in 1907.

According to the report of the U. S. Bureau of Corporations, 195 holders of timberlands own one-quarter of all the standing timber in the United States, and three holders own nearly one-eighth.

The largest single owner in the United States is the Southern Pacific Railroad, with over 100 billion board feet. Three holdings, the Southern Pacific, Weyerhauser, and Northern Pacific, amount to almost 240 billion feet.

The same report tells us that 1694 timber owners hold more than 100 million acres, or something over one-twentieth of the whole land area of the United States.

9 781297 804557